ert,

ience
h

0001064

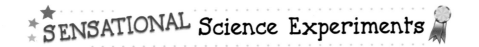

Really Hot Science Projects with Temperature

How Hot Is It?
How Cold Is It?

Robert Gardner

Enslow Publishers, Inc.

40 Industrial Road   PO Box 38
Box 398   Aldershot
Berkeley Heights, NJ 07922 Hants GU12 6BP
USA   UK

http://www.enslow.com

Library of Congress Cataloging-in-Publication Data

Gardner, Robert, 1929–
    Really hot science projects with temperature : how hot is it? how cold is it? / Robert Gardner.
      v. cm. — (Sensational science experiments)
    Includes bibliographical references and index.
    Contents: Heat and temperature — How can you make a thermometer's liquid rise or fall? — Go on a temperature hunt — Moving liquids by temperature difference — What is your temperature? — Temperature and evaporation — Temperatures all day long! — Temperatures above and below ground — Sun, color, and temperature — Sun and seasonal temperatures — Earth, sun, and temperature — Diffusion and temperature — Temperature and chemistry — Temperature and speed of a chemical reaction — How cold can you make water? — The temperature of melting ice or snow — Make your own thermometer — Dew point — Temperature and the greenhouse effect.
  ISBN 0-7660-2015-0
  1. Temperature—Juvenile literature. 2. Heat—Juvenile literature. 3. Cold—Juvenile literature. 4. Science—Experiments—Juvenile literature. [1. Temperature—Experiments. 2. Heat—Experiments. 3. Cold—Experiments. 4. Experiments.] I. Title. II. Series: Gardner, Robert, 1929–   . Sensational science experiments.
QC271.4.G368 2003
536'.078—dc21

2002153849

Printed in the United States of America

10 9 8 7 6 5 4 3 2 1

To Our Readers: We have done our best to make sure all Internet Addresses in this book were active and appropriate when we went to press. However, the author and the publisher have no control over and assume no liability for the material available on those Internet sites or on other Web sites they may link to. Any comments or suggestions can be sent by e-mail to comments@enslow.com or to the address on the back cover.

Illustration credits: Tom LaBaff

Cover illustrations: Tom LaBaff

Contents

(Experiments with a 🎗 symbol feature Ideas for Your Science Fair.)

Introduction

Heat and Temperature

We all know the differences between sipping a hot chocolate and slurping a cold milk shake. The big difference is temperature.

Temperature and heat are not the same. Temperature tells us how hot or cold something is. For example, normal body temperature is about 98.6 degrees Fahrenheit. On the other hand, heat is how much energy one object can give to another. For example, you might find it uncomfortable to sit in a bathtub full of very hot water. A drop of the same water on your hand would not bother you. The temperature of both is the same. But the tub of water can transfer much more heat energy to your body.

We measure temperature with thermometers. The lines and numbers on a thermometer are the scale. People around the world use three different temperature scales. One scale was developed in 1724 by a German physicist, Gabriel Daniel Fahrenheit. People in the United States now use the Fahrenheit scale for measuring the temperature of everyday things, such as the outside air for weather reports and the air in an oven when cooking.

Room temperature on the Fahrenheit scale is about 68 degrees. It can be written as 68°F.

Another scale was developed by Anders Celsius just a few years later, in 1742. His scale was simpler than Fahrenheit's scale because Celsius made the number of degrees between two particular temperature points an even 100. People in most of the world outside the United States use the Celsius scale to measure air temperatures. Room temperature on the Celsius scale is about 20 degrees (20°C).

Scientists all over the world also use the Celsius scale, but they also use a third temperature scale, called the Kelvin scale. The Kelvin scale was developed by a British physicist named William Thomson (Lord Kelvin) in 1848. Room temperature on the Kelvin scale is about 293K.

This book is full of experiments that use thermometers. In one experiment, you can build your own thermometer and develop your own temperature scale.

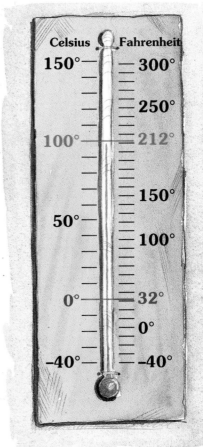

Entering a Science Fair

Some of the experiments in this book might give you ideas for a science fair project. Those experiments are marked with a symbol. Remember, judges at science fairs like experiments that are imaginative. It is hard to be creative unless you are really interested in your project. Pick a subject that you enjoy and want to know more about.

You can add to the value of the experiments you do by keeping notes. Set up an experiment notebook and record your work carefully. As you do some of these experiments, you will think of new questions that you can answer with experiments of your own. Go ahead and carry out these experiments (with your parents' or teacher's permission). You are developing the kind of curiosity that is shared by all scientists.

If you enter a science fair, you should read some of the books listed in the back of this book. They will give you helpful hints and lots of useful information about science fairs. You will learn how to prepare great reports that include charts and graphs. You will also learn how to set up and display your work, how to present your project, and how to talk with judges and visitors.

Safety First

As you do the experiments in this or any other book, do them safely. Remember the rules listed below and follow them closely.

1. Any experiments that you do should be done under the supervision of a parent, teacher, or another adult.

2. Read all instructions carefully. If you have questions, check with an adult. Do not take chances.

3. If you work with a friend who enjoys science too, keep a serious attitude while experimenting. Fooling around can be dangerous to you and to others.

4. Keep the area where you are experimenting clean and organized. When you have finished, clean up and put away the materials you were using.

5. **When doing these experiments, use only non-mercury thermometers, such as those filled with alcohol. The liquid in some thermometers is mercury. It is dangerous to touch mercury or to breathe mercury vapor, and such thermometers have been banned in many states. If you have a mercury thermometer in the house, ask an adult if it can be taken to a local mercury thermometer exchange location.**

Thermometer Liquid

Most household thermometers are used to measure temperature indoors or outdoors. You need one with a colored liquid that is inside a straight, narrow, closed tube. The tube should be connected to a bulb at the base of the thermometer. The bulb holds a larger amount of the liquid. A temperature scale will be marked on or beside the narrow tube. Is the scale in degrees Fahrenheit or Celsius? Some thermometers show both scales. Notice that the lower numbers are closer to the bulb. The higher numbers are farther from the bulb. **Ask an adult** to help you find a thermometer for this experiment.

Let's Get Started!

1. Hold your thumb against the thermometer bulb and watch the liquid in the narrow tube. What happens to the liquid?

2. What do you think will happen to the liquid if you place the thermometer bulb in a stream of water from your cold water tap? Try it! Were you right?

3. What happens to the liquid if you hold it **for a short time** in a stream of water from the hot water tap?

Rises and Falls

④ What happens to the liquid in the thermometer when you place an ice cube on the thermometer bulb?

Based on all your experiments, what happens to the amount of space the colored liquid takes up when it becomes colder? The amount of space is called *volume*. What happens to the liquid's volume when it becomes warmer?

Things you will need:
✔ an ADULT
✔ small indoor or outdoor linear thermometer
✔ hot and cold water taps
✔ ice cube

Go on a

Things you will need:
- ✔ outdoor thermometer
- ✔ home or school
- ✔ outdoor area
- ✔ notebook and pencil

In this experiment, you will go on a temperature hunt. You will look for the warmest and coldest places inside and outside your home or school.

When you take a thermometer into a new place, it takes some time for the liquid inside it to reach its final level. After you move the thermometer, you should wait several minutes before reading the temperature.

Let's Get Started!

1. Begin by using your thermometer to look for the warmest place inside your home or school. During your hunt, see if you can answer these questions: Is it warmer near the floor or the ceiling? Is it warmer near a window or beside an inside wall? Is it warmer inside or outside a closet? If the building you are in has more than one story, is it warmer upstairs or downstairs? Write down the temperature you find in each place.

2. Not counting freezers and refrigerators, what is the coldest place in the building? Do you think your answer will change as the seasons change?

Temperature Hunt

3 Take your temperature hunt outside. Where is it warmest? Where is it coldest? During your hunt, try to answer these questions: Is it warmer in the sun or in the shade? Are the temperatures on the north and south sides of the building different? How about the temperatures on the east and west sides?

Do you think that the time of day affects the temperature? In a later experiment, you will investigate this question.

Moving Liquids by

In the previous experiment, you probably found that air was warmer near the ceiling and cooler near the floor. Liquids, such as water, and gases, such as air, are fluids. Different fluids often act in the same way. Because of this, you can use liquids to see why air is warmer near a ceiling.

Things you will need:
- ✔ 2 clear plastic cups
- ✔ hot tap water
- ✔ food coloring
- ✔ wooden coffee stirrer
- ✔ cold water
- ✔ eyedropper

Let's Get Started!

1. Nearly fill a clear plastic cup with hot tap water. Add several drops of food coloring and stir with a wooden coffee stirrer.

2. Nearly fill a second cup with cold water.

3. Fill an eyedropper with hot colored water from the first cup.

4. Place the end of the eyedropper on the bottom of the cup of cold water. Very gently squeeze a drop of the hot water into the bottom of the cold water. What happens? Does the hot water stay on the bottom of the cup? Or does it move to the top of the cold water?

Temperature Difference

⑤ Repeat the experiment, but this time color the cold water. Use the eyedropper to gently squeeze a drop of colored cold water onto the bottom of a cup of clear hot water. Does the cold water stay on the bottom of the hot water? Or does it move to the top of the hot water?

How does this experiment help you to understand why air near the ceiling is warmer than air near the floor?

Why do you think heaters are usually found near the floor?

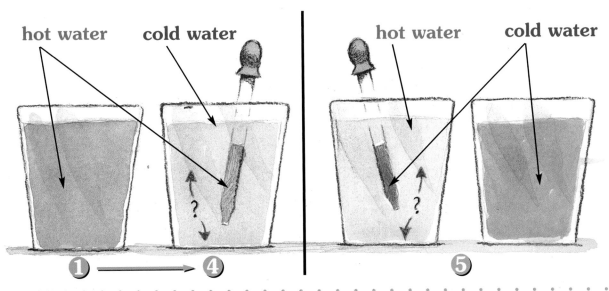

hot water   cold water   hot water   cold water

① ⟶ ④   ⑤

A sk your parent or another adult to show you how to use a digital thermometer that measures body temperatures. For the most accurate reading, the thermometer is placed under the tongue for a period of time. Most digital thermometers give a signal to indicate when the temperature has stopped changing. At that point, the thermometer is removed from the mouth. There will be a digital readout of the temperature on the thermometer.

Let's Get Started!

1 Use the thermometer to find your body temperature when you first wake up. Do it before brushing your teeth or eating. What is your body temperature early in the morning? Write down the time and your temperature on a data table like the one shown.

2 Continue to measure and record your temperature at different times throughout the day until you go to bed. Is your temperature always the same? If not, when is your temperature highest? When is it lowest?

3 Have other people measure their temperatures throughout the day. Do their temperatures change the

Temperature?

way yours does? If not, how are the patterns different?

Ideas for Your Science Fair

Try measuring your temperature before and after exercise. Does exercise change your body temperature? If it does, does it make it higher or lower?

Is your body temperature higher on warm days than on cold days? How do body temperatures compare with air temperatures? Which show greater changes?

Do some research at your library on warm- and cold-blooded animals.

Temperature

You have probably noticed that you feel colder when the wind is blowing. You may have seen weather reports that give the temperature and then the windchill temperature. Does wind make the air cooler?

Let's Get Started!

Things you will need:
- ✔ outdoor thermometer
- ✔ electric fan
- ✔ an ADULT
- ✔ water
- ✔ paper towel
- ✔ notebook and pencil

1. Place a thermometer near an electric fan that is not turned on. You will find out the temperature of the still air near the fan. After several minutes, the thermometer reading will not change anymore. Read the thermometer and record the temperature of the air.

2. Turn on the fan. **Be sure to keep your hands away from the fan. Ask an adult** to hold the thermometer in the moving air. Be sure not to touch the thermometer bulb. What is the temperature of the moving air? Is it less than the temperature of still air? Is air that is moving cooler than still air?

3. Spread a few drops of water over the back of one

and Evaporation

hand. Then hold the backs of both hands in front of the fan blowing air. Which hand feels cooler? From which hand is water evaporating?

4. To see if evaporation really causes a drop in temperature, wrap a folded piece of damp paper towel around the bottom of the thermometer. **Ask an adult** to hold the thermometer in front of the fan. What happens to the temperature? What can you conclude?

Temperatures

For this experiment, choose a day when you can measure temperatures every hour.

Things you will need:
- ✔ thermometer
- ✔ outdoor spot that is shaded all day
- ✔ notebook and pencil
- ✔ clock or watch
- ✔ graph paper

Let's Get Started!

① Put a thermometer outdoors in a place where it will be in the shade all day, such as under a picnic table. As soon as you get up, record that outside temperature. Then try to read the thermometer every hour until you go to bed. Record temperatures and times in a chart like the partial one shown below.

Time (A.M.)	Temperature (°F)	Time (P.M.)	Temperature (°F)
6:05	44	12:40	75
7:30	47	1:45	78
_____	___	_____	___

② The next day, use your chart to make a graph. Plot temperature on the vertical (up-and-down) lines, and times on the horizontal (side-to-side) lines. (In the sample graph, you can see that at 9:00 A.M. the temperature was about 56°F.)

At what time did you record the highest

All Day Long!

temperature? At what time did you record the lowest temperature?

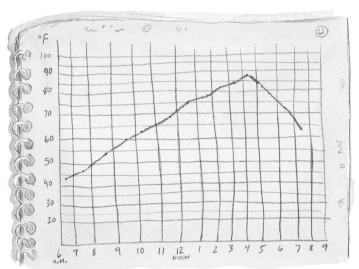

3 Look at your graph very carefully. How can you tell over what time period the temperature was increasing fastest? Slowest? How can you tell over what time period the temperature was decreasing fastest? Slowest?

How does your graph compare with the one shown? How are they the same? How are they different?

You probably found that the temperature was coldest early in the morning. That is not always true, but usually it is. Can you explain why?

Idea for Your Science Fair

Repeat the experiment on other days. Are the warmest and coolest times approximately the same each day?

Temperatures Above

Repeat the previous experiment, but this time measure temperatures underground as well as above ground.

**Let's Get Started!**

1. Put a thermometer outdoors where it will be shaded all day, such as under a picnic table.

2. Put a second thermometer in a small box. In the same shady area, ask permission to bury the box and thermometer underground. Use a spade to cut out a square piece of sod about 6 inches on a side and about 4 inches deep. Remove the sod in one piece. Place the box with the thermometer in the hollow space. Then replace the sod.

3. Read and write down the temperatures on both thermometers every hour from early morning until you go to bed. You will have to carefully remove and replace the chunk of sod each time you read the thermometer that is underground. Record temperatures and times in a chart like the partial one shown on the next page.

Time (A.M.)	Temperature (°F)		Time (P.M.)	Temperature (°F)	
	air	ground		air	ground
6:05	35	40	12:40	60	46
7:10	42	41	1:45	64	47
___	___	___	___	___	___

❹ Just as you did in the previous experiment, use the information to make a graph. Mark the air and underground temperatures at the times you made your measurements. You can plot both sets of temperatures, in different colors, on the same graph. What, if anything, can you conclude from your experiment?

Idea for Your Science Fair

How does the depth beneath the ground affect temperature readings during the day?

Have you ever wondered why people who live in hot, sunny climates wear light-colored clothes? Have you noticed how warm you feel when you stand in front of a sunny window wearing a dark shirt?

Let's Get Started!

1. To see how temperatures are affected by color, you will need two identical small, shiny tin cans. Paint one of the cans, both inside and outside, with flat black paint.

2. When the paint has thoroughly dried, place the cans side by side in front of a bright, sunny window. Place a thermometer in each can. After about twenty minutes, read both thermometers. In which can is the temperature higher?

Things you will need:
- ✔ 2 identical small, shiny tin cans
- ✔ flat black paint
- ✔ bright sunshine
- ✔ 2 outdoor thermometers
- ✔ clock or watch
- ✔ a cup
- ✔ cold water

3. Pour a small cup of cold water into each can. Use a thermometer to make sure that the temperature of the water in the two cans is nearly the same.

4. Again, place the cans side by side in front of a bright, sunny window. Which can do you think will have the

Temperature

higher temperature an hour later? Try it! Was your prediction correct?

Idea for Your Science Fair

You can experiment with clothing as well. Wrap thermometers in different colored clothing of about the same weight. Place the clothing samples in bright sunlight for about twenty minutes. Which article of clothing do you think will be warmest? Which do you think will be coolest? Open the clothes and check the thermometers. Which one was warmest? Which was coolest? Were they the ones you predicted?

Sun and Seasonal

In general, air temperatures are lower in winter than in summer. You may have noticed that the sun is lower in the sky during winter. Also, the time between sunrise and sunset is shorter in winter than in summer. The sun is Earth's only outside source of heat. We can expect differences in seasonal temperatures to be related to the sun.

Let's Get Started!

1. On a sunny fall, winter, or spring day, turn a thermometer toward the sun. **Do not look directly at the sun. It can damage your eyes!** Hold the thermometer so that it faces the sun, as shown in the drawing. Keep the thermometer in this position until the temperature does not change anymore.

Things you will need:
✓ sunshine
✓ outdoor thermometer
✓ notebook and pencil

2. Write down the temperature.

3. Now turn the thermometer so that it casts a very small shadow. The shadow should be as small as possible. Again, keep the thermometer in this position until the temperature does not change anymore. Record this temperature.

Temperatures

④ Compare the two temperatures you have recorded. What can you conclude?

Ideas for Your Science Fair

Many people think summer occurs when Earth is closer to the sun. This is not true. Earth is approximately 148 million kilometers (92 million miles) from the sun on January 1. It is 153 million kilometers (95 million miles) from the sun on July 1.

Why do you think temperatures are higher in summer than in winter?

Earth, Sun, and

Earth is closer to the sun in winter than it is in summer. How can we be colder in the winter if we are closer to the sun? To see why, use a flashlight to represent the sun and a globe to represent Earth.

Let's Get Started!

1. Hold the flashlight so that its circular beam points directly onto the tropic of Capricorn. It is the line that goes around the globe 23.5 degrees south of the equator. On the first day of winter, the sun is directly above the tropic of Capricorn.

2. Move the flashlight upward without changing the angle of its beam until its light falls on the United States. As you can see, the light shining on the United States is not circular. The beam is spread out over a much bigger surface.

   During winter, the sunlight reaching the United States is spread over more surface. Therefore, the light is not as strong and cannot provide as much heat.

Things you will need:
- ✔ flashlight
- ✔ globe that shows tropic of Capricorn and tropic of Cancer

Temperature

③ Move the flashlight so that it points directly at the tropic of Cancer. This is the line on the globe that is 23.5 degrees north of the equator. On the first day of summer, the sun is directly over the tropic of Cancer. Again, without changing the angle of the beam, move the flashlight upward until its light falls on the United States. As you can see, the light is much less spread out, or more concentrated, than it was when the winter "sunlight" fell on it.

Diffusion and

All matter is made up of molecules—the smallest entire pieces of a substance. Molecules are always moving. Sometimes they separate and spread out. You can find this out for yourself.

Let's Get Started!

1. Have a friend open a bottle of perfume and place it on a table a few feet from where you are standing. After a few minutes, you will be able to smell the perfume. In order for you to smell the perfume's odor, the molecules of perfume must have moved through the air to your nose. The spreading out of matter in this way is called diffusion.

2. To see how temperature affects diffusion, nearly fill a drinking glass with very cold water. Fill a second glass to the same level with hot water. Add a drop of green or blue food coloring to the cold water. Then add a drop of the same food coloring to the hot water. Watch the color diffuse in both glasses. In which glass does the food coloring diffuse faster?

3. Repeat the experiment, but this time drop a few crystals of a cherry-flavored drink mix into the cold

Temperature

water. Then drop a few of the same crystals into the hot water. Place the glass of cold water in a refrigerator. Leave the glass of hot water in a warm room. Watch the crystals diffuse over a period of days. Do they diffuse faster in warm or in cold water? What can you conclude about the effect of temperature on diffusion?

Things you will need:
- ✔ a friend
- ✔ bottle of perfume
- ✔ 2 drinking glasses
- ✔ hot and cold water
- ✔ green or blue food coloring
- ✔ cherry-flavored powdered drink mix
- ✔ refrigerator

Temperature

Sometimes substances that are mixed together change to form one or more new substances. A chemical change has taken place. The rusting of iron is an example of a chemical change. The burning of wood, natural gas, and coal are other chemical changes. When a substance dissolves (disappears) in water, we say that a solution has formed. For example, sugar dissolves when added to hot tea. The temperature can increase or decrease during a chemical change or during dissolving. If the temperature decreases, the change is said to be endothermic (taking in heat). If the temperature increases, the change is said to be exothermic (giving out heat).

Let's Get Started!

1. Add 100 mL of water to a drinking glass. Measure the temperature of the water.

2. Add two tablespoons of Epsom salts to the water and stir to dissolve the solid. Measure the temperature of the solution. Is the dissolving of Epsom salts endothermic or exothermic?

③ Place a large tea cup in a sink. Add 100 mL of 3% hydrogen peroxide. Measure the temperature of the liquid.

④ Add a small packet of dry yeast to the hydrogen peroxide and stir. What evidence is there that a chemical reaction is taking place? The gas making the foam is oxygen. Use a teaspoon to push away some of the foam. Then measure the temperature of the liquid again. Is the reaction of yeast with hydrogen peroxide endothermic or exothermic?

Things you will need:
- ✔ metric measuring cup
- ✔ water
- ✔ drinking glass
- ✔ thermometer
- ✔ tablespoon
- ✔ Epsom salts
- ✔ tea cup
- ✔ sink
- ✔ bottle of 3% hydrogen peroxide
- ✔ dry yeast
- ✔ teaspoon

Temperature and Speed

Things you will need:
✓ 2 drinking glasses
✓ hot and cold tap water
✓ 2 identical seltzer tablets

In the experiment about diffusion you learned that matter is made up of molecules. The molecules are always moving. Scientists have learned that the temperature of a substance is related to the speed of its molecules. The faster they move, the higher the temperature. They also know that chemical changes take place when molecules of different substances bump into one another. How do you think temperature will affect the speed of a chemical change?

Let's Get Started!

1. Fill a drinking glass about halfway with cold tap water. Fill a second glass with the same amount of hot tap water.

2. Drop a seltzer tablet into the cold water. At exactly the same time, drop a second seltzer tablet into the hot water. The fizzing that you see is the result of a chemical reaction between substances in the tablets.

One product of the reaction is carbon dioxide gas. It is the gas that makes up the tiny bubbles you see as the fizz.

In which glass does the reaction go faster? Did you guess right? Why do you think you were right or wrong?

cold   **hot**

How Cold Can You

1 Pour cold water into a small plastic cup. Put a laboratory thermometer into the cup. You can probably borrow a laboratory thermometer from your school's science teacher. There should be enough water in the cup to more than cover the thermometer bulb, but it should not come too high up the thermometer. Write down the temperature of the water.

2 Put the cup of water with the thermometer into a freezer. You may need to support the thermometer so that it stands up. Record the temperature of the water and the time every ten minutes. At what temperature do you notice ice beginning to form?

> Things you will need:
> ✔ cold tap water
> ✔ small plastic cup
> ✔ small laboratory thermometer
> ✔ notebook and pencil
> ✔ freezer
> ✔ clock or watch
> ✔ graph paper

3 Once ice starts to form, check the temperature every fifteen minutes. In your notebook, record the time and the temperature every time you read the thermometer. What happens to the temperature of the freezing water?

Make Water Ice?

Continue recording temperatures and times until the water is completely frozen and the temperature no longer decreases. What is the temperature when it no longer changes? Why does the water not get any colder? Leave the thermometer and ice in the freezer for the next experiment.

④ Use the temperatures you have recorded to draw a graph. Show time along the horizontal (side-to-side) axis and temperatures along the vertical (up-and-down) axis. Does your graph look like the one shown? In this graph, what is happening during the sections of the graph marked A, B, and C?

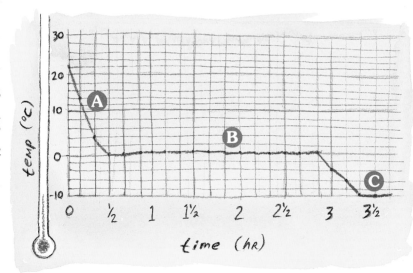

Idea for Your Science Fair

Do some research at your library. What is the coldest possible temperature?

In the previous experiment, you found the freezing temperature of water. It was probably about 0°C or 32°F. You might think that ice or snow, which is made of tiny ice crystals, will melt at the same temperature.

Let's Get Started!

1 Open the freezer and remove the cup of ice and the thermometer you used in the previous experiment. Place the cup and thermometer in a protected place in a warm room. Using an indoor thermometer, measure the temperature of the room.

2 Check the temperature of the ice every ten minutes until it melts and reaches the temperature of the room. Record the numbers in your notebook.

At what temperatures does the temperature remain the same for a long time? What do you think is the reason for these periods of constant temperature? (See page 47 for an explanation.)

3 Does the amount of ice or snow affect the melting temperature? To find out, you will need to put some finely crushed ice or snow into a cup. Stir the ice or snow gently with the thermometer until the

Melting Ice or Snow

temperature stops changing. What is the temperature of the melting ice or snow?

④ Fill a bucket with melting ice or snow. Again, gently stir the melting ice or snow with a thermometer. Does the amount of ice or snow affect the temperature at which it melts?

Ideas for Your Science Fair

How cold would it have to be for the liquid in a thermometer to freeze if the liquid were isopropyl alcohol?

How does a gas thermometer work?

Things you will need:
- ✔ cup of ice and thermometer used in the previous experiment
- ✔ warm room
- ✔ indoor thermometer
- ✔ clock or watch
- ✔ notebook and pencil
- ✔ finely crushed ice or snow
- ✔ cup
- ✔ bucket

37

Make Your Own

You can make a simple thermometer of your own.

Let's Get Started!

1. Fill a large test tube to the top with water.

2. Coat one end of a clear drinking straw with petroleum jelly. Push that end of the straw through the hole in a rubber stopper. If you do not have a rubber stopper, use some modeling clay to make a plug.

3. Push the rubber stopper or clay plug firmly into the mouth of the test tube. The water should rise about halfway up the drinking straw.

4. Let the test tube stand in an empty drinking glass for ten minutes. Then mark the water level on the straw with a marking pen.

5. Put the test tube in a glass of hot tap water. What happens to the water

Things you will need:
- ✔ large test tube
- ✔ water
- ✔ clear drinking straw
- ✔ petroleum jelly
- ✔ 1-hole rubber stopper to fit test tube, or modeling clay
- ✔ 3 drinking glasses
- ✔ clock or watch
- ✔ marking pen
- ✔ hot and cold tap water
- ✔ ruler

level in the straw? Mark the water level with the marking pen.

6 Put the test tube in a glass of cold water. What happens to the water level in the straw? Use the marker to mark this level.

What happens to the volume of water (the amount of space it takes up) when it gets hotter? When it gets colder?

7 Use a ruler and marker to divide the spaces between your marks into equal degrees. Number the degrees. You can name your new temperature scale after yourself!

Idea for Your Science Fair
With an adult to help you, carry out an experiment to show what happens to the volume of air when it is heated or cooled.

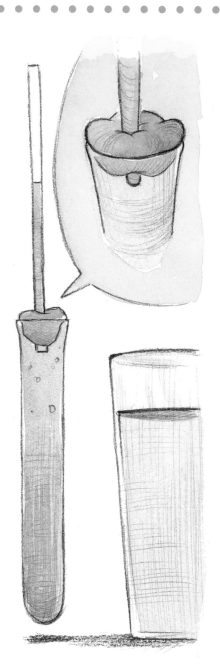

Measuring

Just as sugar dissolves in water, so water dissolves in air. More water can dissolve in hot air than in cold air. As air cools, which often happens at night, water leaves the air. Dew forms. You have probably seen dew on grass or cars in the early morning. In the summer, dew droplets may appear on a cold drink container.

You may have heard the words *dew point* on weather reports. Dew point is a temperature, the temperature at which dew begins to form. To make that clear, we will refer to it as the dew point temperature. You can find this temperature by experimenting.

Let's Get Started!

1. Use a thermometer to measure the room temperature.

2. Fill a shiny metal can about halfway with warm water. Put the thermometer into the water. Write down the water's temperature.

3. Slowly lower the temperature of the water. To do this, add small pieces of ice as you gently stir with the thermometer. Watch the outside of the can. When

Dew Point

you see dew (moisture) forming on the can, write down the water temperature. You have reached the dew point temperature for the conditions in the room.

Ideas for Your Science Fair

Find the dew points at different times of the year. During which season are dew points highest? Lowest? During which season of the year is the air driest inside your home or school?

How are dew points related to humidity?

Temperature and

Have you been in a greenhouse at a nursery or garden store? Greenhouses are warm and bright inside to make plants grow faster. The glass reflects some of the sun's heat back into the greenhouse. Earth receives huge amounts of heat from the sun. If Earth kept all that heat, it would be too hot for life. However, without some of the heat, Earth would be too cold for life. Our atmosphere of air prevents such extreme temperatures. During daylight, Earth's atmosphere absorbs about half the sun's energy. It reflects the rest back into space. At night, gases in the atmosphere act like the glass in a greenhouse. They trap heat that would otherwise escape and reflect it back down to Earth.

You can see the greenhouse effect for yourself.

 Let's Get Started!

1 Find two identical shoe boxes. Use clear tape to fasten thermometers to the bottom of each box as shown in the drawing. Use small pieces of cardboard to shade the thermometer bulbs from the sun. Cover the top of one box with plastic wrap. Seal the plastic securely to

the Greenhouse Effect

the box with masking tape so that air cannot escape or enter. Leave the other box uncovered.

2 Put the boxes in the sun until the temperatures in both stop changing. In which box is the temperature higher? What can you conclude?

Ideas for Your Science Fair

Design an experiment to show that the greenhouse effect occurs in automobiles.

Do some library or Internet research. Find out how the greenhouse effect may change Earth's average temperature. What gas do scientists think may cause this change?

Words to Know

Celsius temperature scale—A temperature scale developed in 1742 by Anders Celsius, a Swedish astronomer who lived from 1701 to 1744.

chemical change—The combination of two or more different substances to form one or more new substances.

diffusion—The spreading out of a substance due to the motion of molecules.

endothermic—The quality of absorbing heat, causing a decrease in surrounding temperature.

equator—An imaginary line circling the globe that divides Earth into northern and southern hemispheres.

evaporation—The change of a liquid to a gas with or without the addition of heat.

exothermic—The quality of releasing heat, causing an increase in surrounding temperature.

Fahrenheit temperature scale—A temperature scale developed in 1724 by Gabriel Daniel Fahrenheit, a German physicist who lived from 1686 to 1736.

matter—Anything that takes up space.

molecule—The smallest particle of a substance that has the properties of that substance.

tropic of Cancer—An imaginary line that goes around the globe parallel to the equator but 23.5 degrees, or approximately 2,600 kilometers (1,600 miles), north of the equator. On the first day of summer in the United States, the sun is directly above the tropic of Cancer.

tropic of Capricorn—An imaginary line that goes around the globe parallel to the equator but 23.5 degrees, or approximately 2,600 kilometers (1,600 miles), south of the equator. On the first day of winter in the United States, the sun is directly above the tropic of Capricorn.

volume—The amount of space something takes up.

Further Reading

Benhoff, Susan. *Measurement*. Greensboro, N.C.: Carson-Dellosa Publishing Company, Inc., 1998.

Bombaugh, Ruth. *Science Fair Success, Revised and Expanded*. Springfield, N.J.: Enslow Publishers, Inc., 1999.

Cole, Joanna. *The Magic School Bus in the Arctic: A Book About Heat*. New York: Scholastic, Inc., 1998.

Lafferty, Peter. *Heat and Cold*. Tarrytown, N.Y.: Marshall Cavendish Corporation, 1995.

Ramsay, Helena. *Hot and Cold*. Danbury, Conn.: Children's Press, 1998.

Wood, Robert W. *Heat Fundamentals*. Broomall, Pa.: Chelsea House Publishers, 1999.

Internet Addresses

The Exploratorium. *The Science Explorer*.
  <http://www.exploratorium.edu/science_
  explorer/>

Mercury Fever Thermometers
  <http://www.epa.gov/glnpo/bnsdocs/hg/
  thermometers.html>

Yahooligans!—Science and Nature Experiments
  and Activities
  <http://www.yahooligans.com/Science_and_
  Nature/Experiments_and_Activities/>

Answer to question on page 36:
The temperature stays the same for a long time at about 0°C (32°F) and at the final temperature you recorded. The temperature of melting ice or freezing water, which is 0°C, does not change while the ice melts or freezes. The final temperature is the temperature of the room, which remains quite constant as long as it is controlled by heating or air conditioning units.

Index